THE Cartoon Faces BOOK

Robert Ainsworth

SCHOLASTIC INC.

New York   Toronto   London   Auckland   Sydney
Mexico City   New Delhi   Hong Kong   Buenos Aires

DEDICATED TO
ALL MY OLD SCHOOL FRIENDS – AND ENEMIES

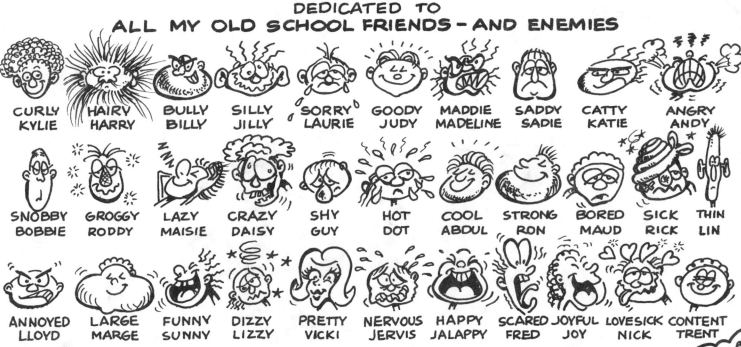

CURLY KYLIE · HAIRY HARRY · BULLY BILLY · SILLY JILLY · SORRY LAURIE · GOODY JUDY · MADDIE MADELINE · SADDY SADIE · CATTY KATIE · ANGRY ANDY

SNOBBY BOBBIE · GROGGY RODDY · LAZY MAISIE · CRAZY DAISY · SHY GUY · HOT DOT · COOL ABDUL · STRONG RON · BORED MAUD · SICK RICK · THIN LIN

ANNOYED LLOYD · LARGE MARGE · FUNNY SUNNY · DIZZY LIZZY · PRETTY VICKI · NERVOUS JERVIS · HAPPY JALAPPY · SCARED FRED · JOYFUL JOY · LOVESICK NICK · CONTENT TRENT

CONTENTS

MORE CONTENTS INSIDE THIS CONTENTED DUDE!

ANY CRUMBS LEFT?

ABOUT THIS BOOK

This simple book is for simple people who simply can't draw for nuts!

By the time you've finished reading it, you'll be able to draw much more than simple nuts . . .you'll be able to draw complicated ones, too!

LOOKS LIKE A GOOD BOOK TA ME!

'SPECIALLY IF I'M IN IT!

HAVE FUN! *Robert Ainsworth*

A NUT FOR A NUT?

YEAH, TA!

How to use this book

I've designed this book so that it's easy for you to locate an example of what you want to draw.

For instance, let's say you want to draw a **smiling** face:

- you can go straight to the *Index* (which is at the back of the book) and look up **smiling**, **or**
- you can look in the *Contents* page (which is at the front of the book) and find the **Face Expressions** pages.

It's as simple as that!

There are also lots of other pages of helpful tips you can find just by browsing through the book.

HOWDY, FOLKS!

DUH! ME THINKS ME LIKES DIS BOOK, ALREADY!

IF ONLY I COULD READ DA WORDS!

COOL!

EVEN I CAN DO IT!

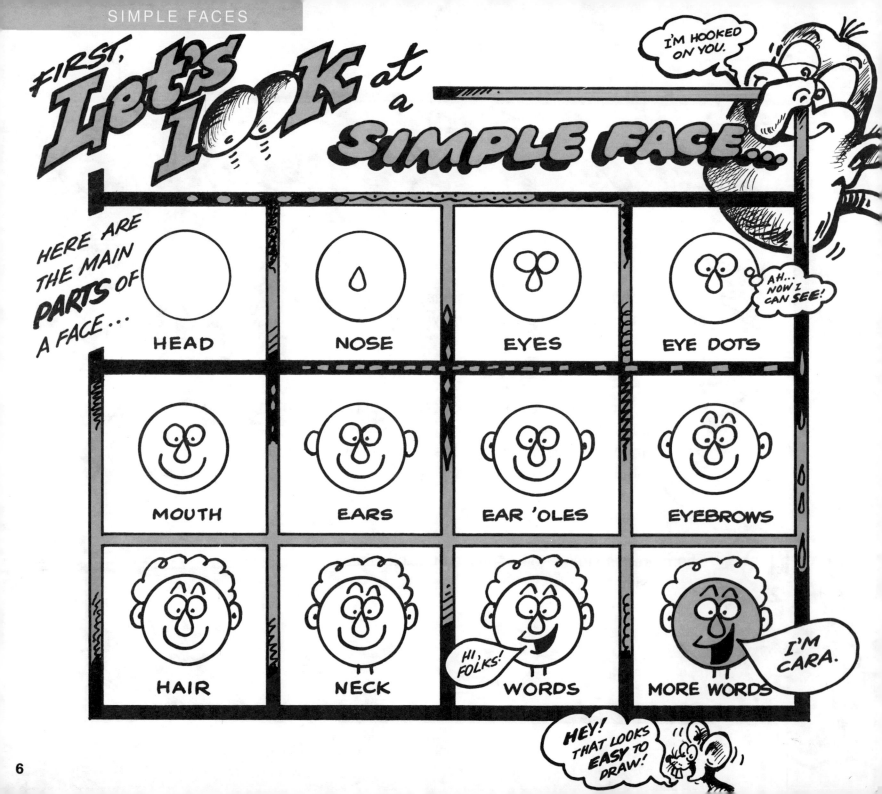

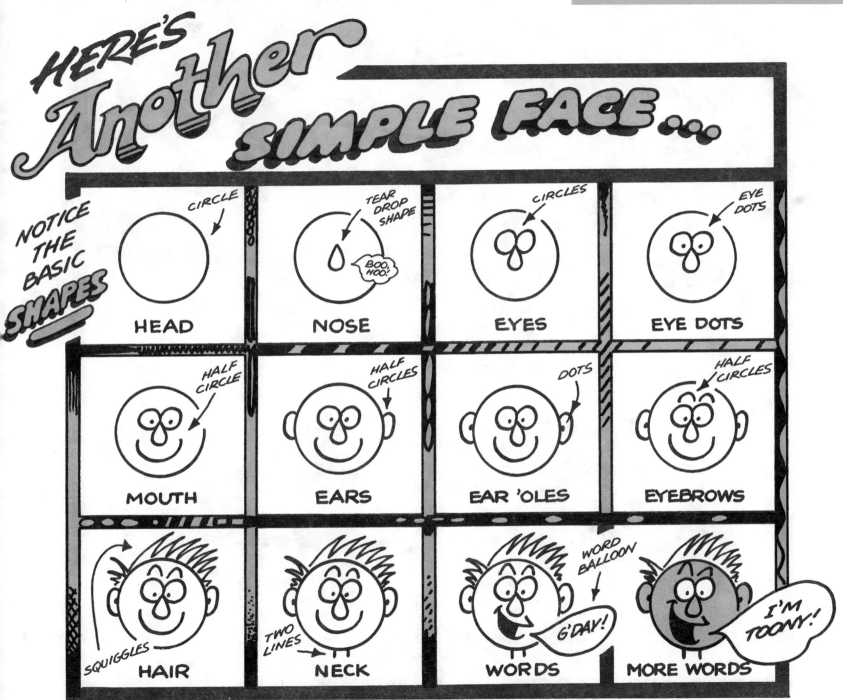

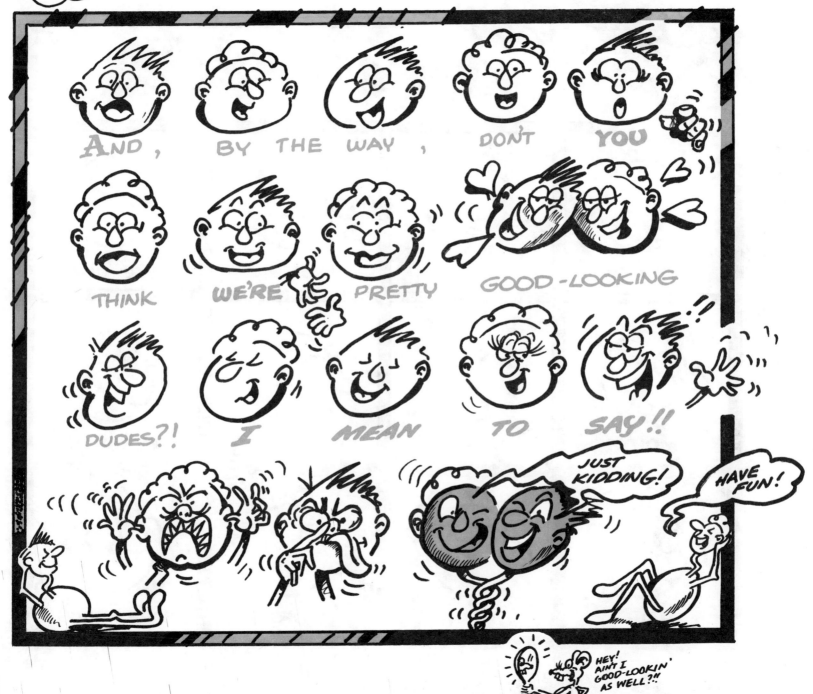

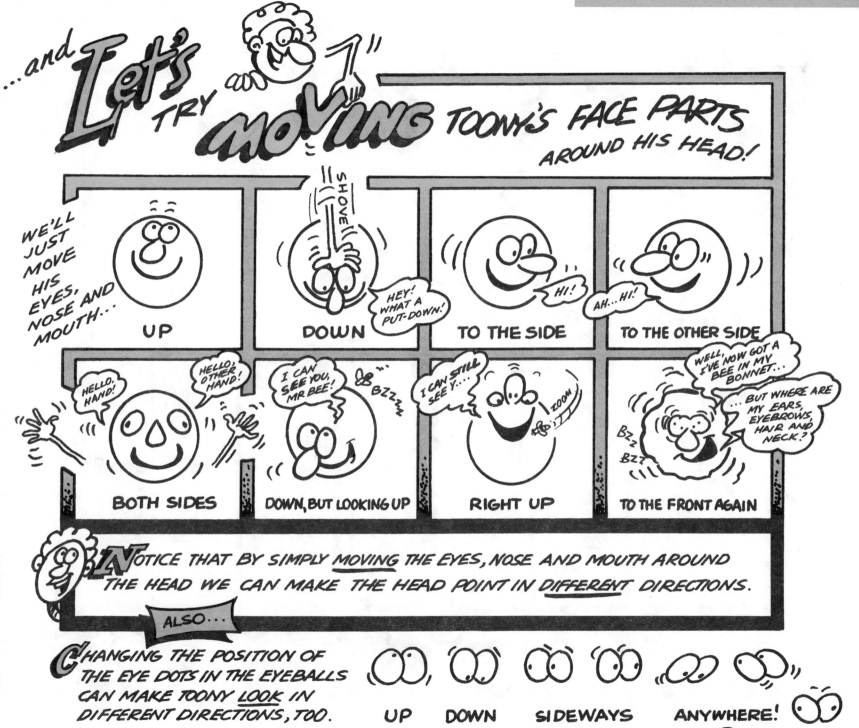

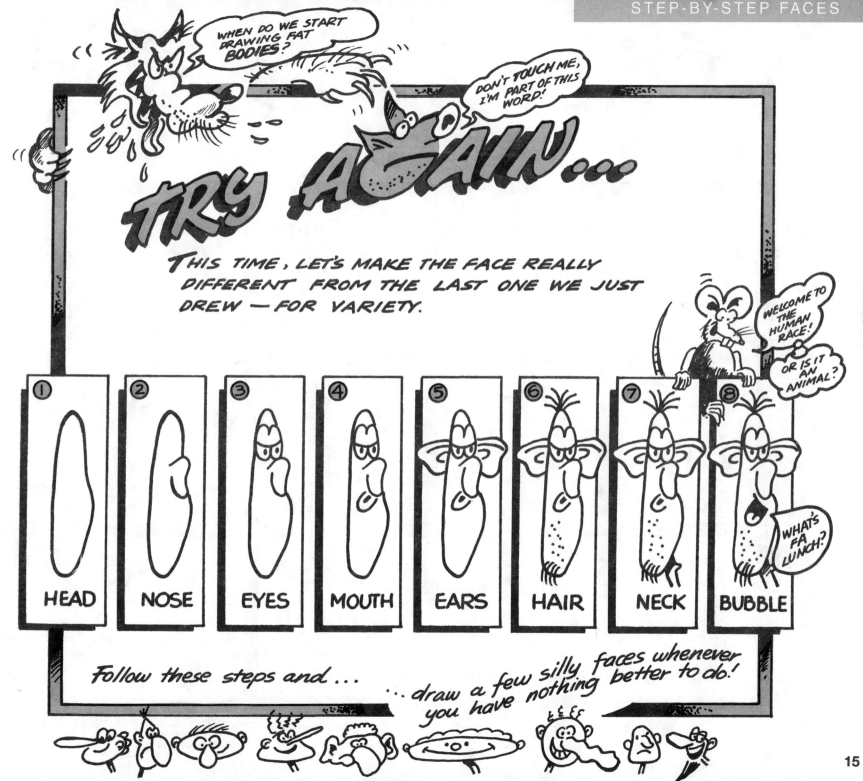

NOW Let's LOOK at NOSES!

I CAN'T SEE PAST BY DOSE!

I'M BEING BEATEN BY A NOSE!

WHO NOSE WHERE I'M GOING?

TRY THESE ON FOR SIZE!

OUCH!

LONG

THAT'S BETTER!

SHORT

WATCH OUT!

BIG!

JUST RIGHT!

SMALL

HINT

TRACE AROUND A COIN FOR THE HEAD SHAPE, FIRST.

① ② ③ RUB OUT

GOOD FOR FISHING WITH!

HOOKED

I'M CUTE.

TURNED UP

TEE! HEE!

A CHIP OFF THE OLD BLOCK!

POINTED

GOOD FOR BULLDOZING SAND HEAPS!

BLUNT

GOOD FOR HANGING SIGNS ON!

KEEP OUT!

HOOKED & TURNED UP

GOOD FOR BLOWING OUT LOTS OF HOT AIR!!

GRR! GRR!

FLARED (ANGRY)

PECK PECK

HEY!

LONG & SKINNY

WE'RE ALWAYS GETTING PICKED ON.

HOW ABOUT "CURLY"?!

DOUBLE!

HOW ABOUT A DUEL?

GOOD FOR TAKING OUT CORKS!

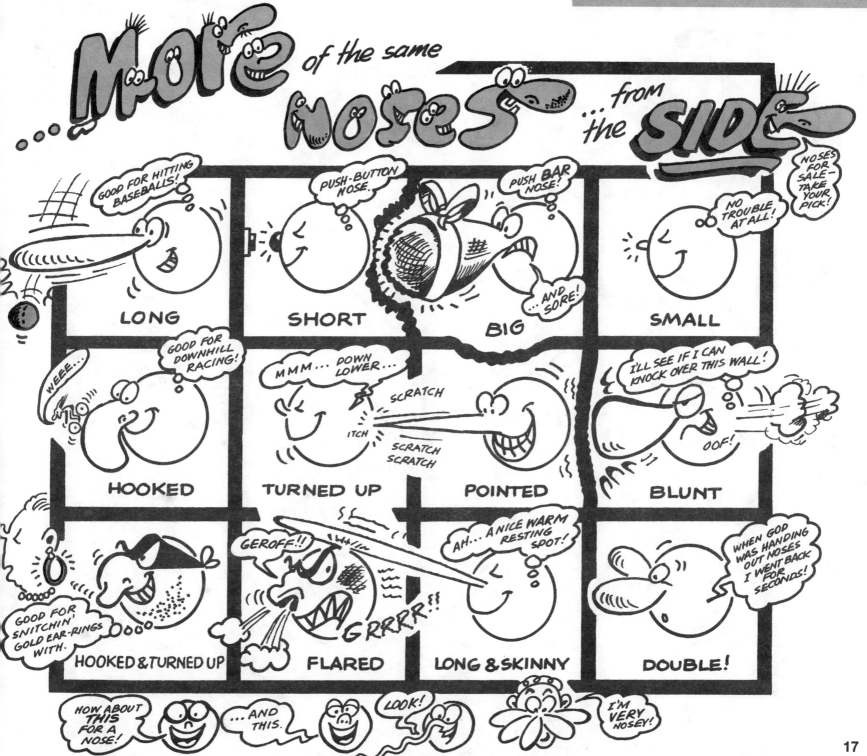

LOOK AT THE... **TYPES** of **eyes** you can use for your **CARTOON CHARACTERS**

CARTOONISTS HAVE THEIR FAVOURITE TYPES OF EYES THAT THEY USE FOR THEIR CHARACTERS!

HERE ARE MOST OF THE TYPES...

DOTS

SQUIGGLES

DOTS & CURVES (SIDES)

DOTS & CURVES (TOP & BOTTOM)

DOTS & LINES

DOTS & SLITS

DOTS & CIRCLES (APART)

DOTS & CIRCLES (OVERLAPPING)

DOTS & OVALS (JOINED)

DOTS & OVALS (SEPARATE)

DOTS, OVALS & CURVE (DOWN)

DOTS, OVALS & CURVE (UP)

EYE LID

EYE LASHES

EYE LID

EYE LASHES

I SPY WITH MY BIG EYES...

YUM!

18

LOOK! **More TYPES of EYES**

DOTS & DOUBLE OVALS

SMALL CIRCLES

DOTS, JOINED CIRCLES, LINE

DOTS, CIRCLES, LINE, CURVES

GLASSES

CIRCLES, CURVES

GLASSES & EYES

DOTS, CIRCLES, CURVES

SMILING, LAUGHING

CURVES (UP)

ASLEEP

ZZZZZZZ

CURVES (DOWN)

CLOSED (SHY OR PLEASED)

ARROWS

HALF SHUT

DOTS, ½ CIRCLES, LINE

WIDE AWAKE

DOTS, BIG CIRCLES

AH, NORMAL AT LAST!

NORMAL EYES

WITH EYELASHES

OR

EYES FEELIN' DIZZY— EYES AM!

19

More MOUTHS ...from the SIDE

JUST A CURVE
- I'M JUST THINKING.
- I'M CATCHING FLIES.

TWO CURVES
- I'M AT THE DENTIST'S.

THREE CURVES
- DR O. PEN WIDE.
- TOP TEETH

THREE CURVES
- DR O. PEN
- FILL IN THE INSIDE OF THE MOUTH
- I'M STILL AT THE DENTISTS.

WIDE OPEN
- DR O.
- I WONDER HOW LONG I HAVE TO KEEP MY MOUTH OPEN!
- TOP AND BOTTOM TEETH AND TONGUE

SHUT
- SKOOL
- I'M NOT THINKING ANYTHING!

SHUT TIGHT
- PRINCIPAL OFFICE
- I'M NOT SAYING ANYTHING!

I'M TALKING.
- POLICE STATION

TALKING WITH TEETH
- I'M A SPARE SET OF TEETH!
- I'M TALKING THROUGH MY BACK TEETH.

TALKING WITH TEETH, TONGUE
- I'M A JACK-IN-THE-BOX!
- I'M A CIRCULAR CHATTER-BOX.

LIPS
- I'M ABOUT TO KISS YOU!

LIPS OPEN
- HOW DO YOU LIKE MY LIPSTICK?

HOW DO YOU LIKE MY LIPSTICK?
SUPER GLUE

21

EARS
SPUD GROWING 'ERE.
'EAR YE! 'EAR YE! EARS FOR SALE— EARS FOR SALE!
NEAT!
SMALL
COOL!
ESPECIALLY WHEN I FLAP 'EM.
LARGE
GOOD FOR UNDER TEACHER'S CHIN!
POINTY
WHA...!?
HELLO!
SSS
FLAPPY
GOOD FOR SAYING GOODBYE!
SEEYA!
STICKY OUTY
WELL PADDED!
FATTY
BATMAN!
GROOVY!
I'M IN THE DOGHOUSE.
FIDO
DROOPY
GOOD FA GETTIN' UP YA NOSE!
SCOOBYDOOPY!
ALL THE BETTER TO HEAR YOU WITH MY DEAR!
STUPY
AT LEAST IT'S NOT ME FEET I'M DRAGGIN'!
SLEEPY
NIRVANA!!
SPACED-OUT

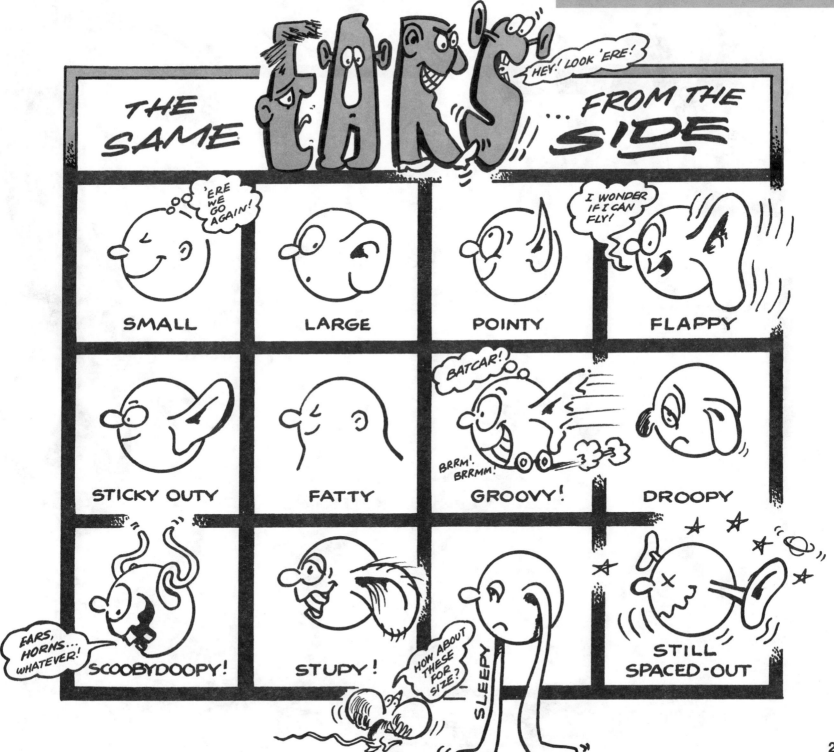

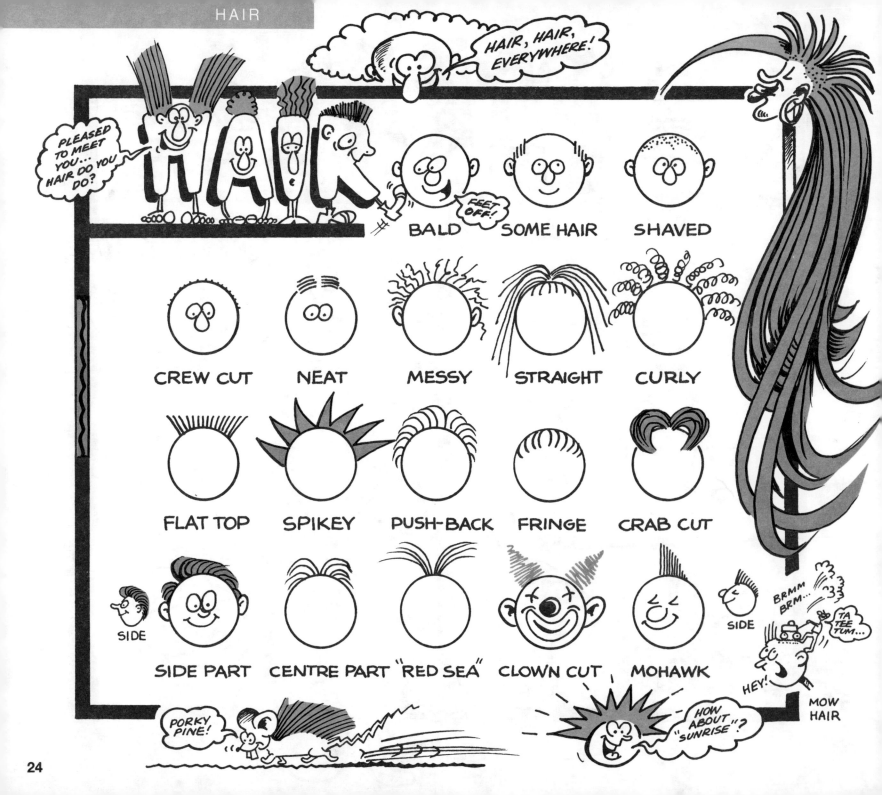

BALD   SOME HAIR   SHAVED

CREW CUT   NEAT   MESSY   STRAIGHT   CURLY

FLAT TOP   SPIKEY   PUSH-BACK   FRINGE   CRAB CUT

SIDE   SIDE PART   CENTRE PART   "RED SEA"   CLOWN CUT   MOHAWK   SIDE   MOW HAIR

MORE HAIR!

COO!

SINGLE! — LONG — SHORT — PAGEBOY — BUN — SIDE

RINGLETS — FRIGHTFUL! — A FRIGHT! — TIGHT CURLS — TOPKNOT

PLAIT — PLAITS — LEANING TOWERS OF PIZZA — SNORK SNORK — PIGTAILS — NEIGH NEIGH — PONYTAIL — SIDE

SPRING LOADED — ABSENT MINDED PROFESSOR — SPOUT! — DREADLOCKS — AFRO

DON'T FORGET US OLD HIPPIES!

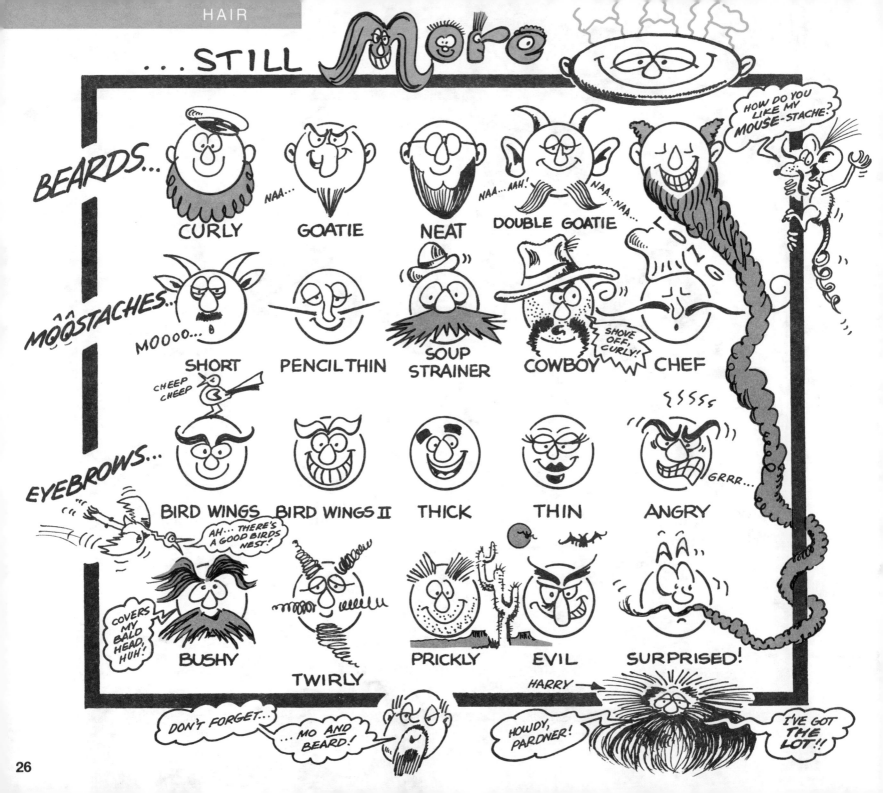

Extras... FACE, HEAD & HAIR DECORATIONS

GET REAL! BUY "X" BRAND OF MAKE-UP!!

BIT NOISY IN THE OLD EAR-OLE!

TRY KISSING ME!

COME WITH ME, YOU!!

OI!

CLANG! CLANG!

MAKE-UP

EARRINGS

NOSE-RINGS

EYEBROW RING

HELLO... I'VE BEEN TRYING TO RING YOU!

STRUTH! THITH HURTTH!

NO BRAINS!

THEY COME IN FIVE DIFFERENT SIZES, TOO.

LIP-RING

TONGUE-RINGS

HEAD-RING

NECK BOLT

NOW, WHERE ARE MY GLASSES?

EYEGLASSES

MORE EYEGLASSES

NECKLACE

HAIR COMB/PIN

A NICE SAFE PLACE FOR MY SAFETY PIN!

27

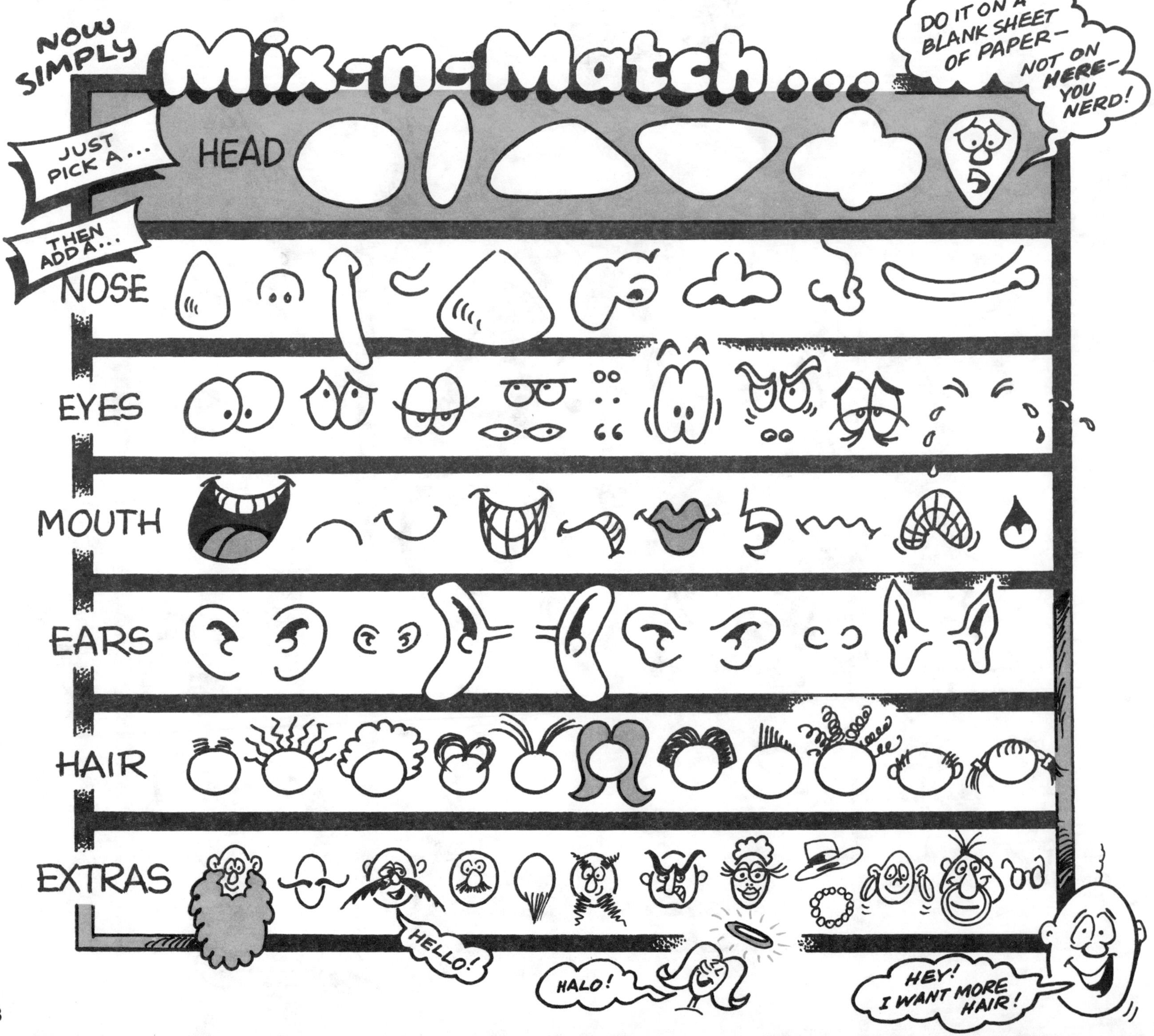
NOW SIMPLY
Mix-n-Match...
DO IT ON A BLANK SHEET OF PAPER— NOT ON HERE— YOU NERD!
JUST PICK A...
HEAD
THEN ADD A...
NOSE
EYES
MOUTH
EARS
HAIR
EXTRAS
HELLO!
HALO!
HEY! I WANT MORE HAIR!

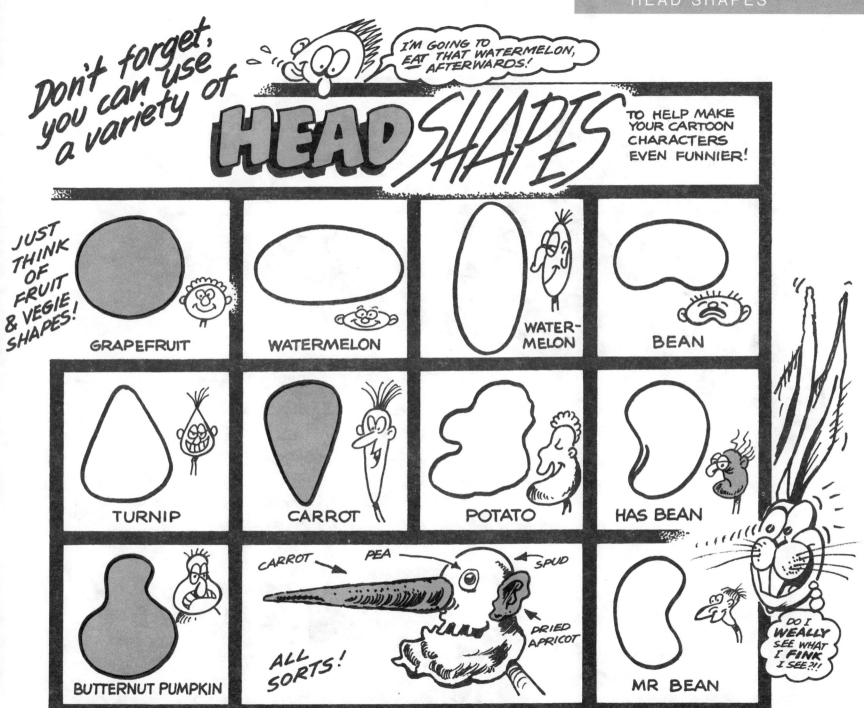

Now we'll take a good look at... FACE EXPRESSIONS

On the next few pages we've drawn lots of face expressions showing people's EMOTIONS, such as HAPPINESS, SADNESS, ANGER, SHYNESS, ETC.

There are TWO faces for each emotion: one from the FRONT — and one from the SIDE.

Use these expressions to help make your cartoons come ALIVE!

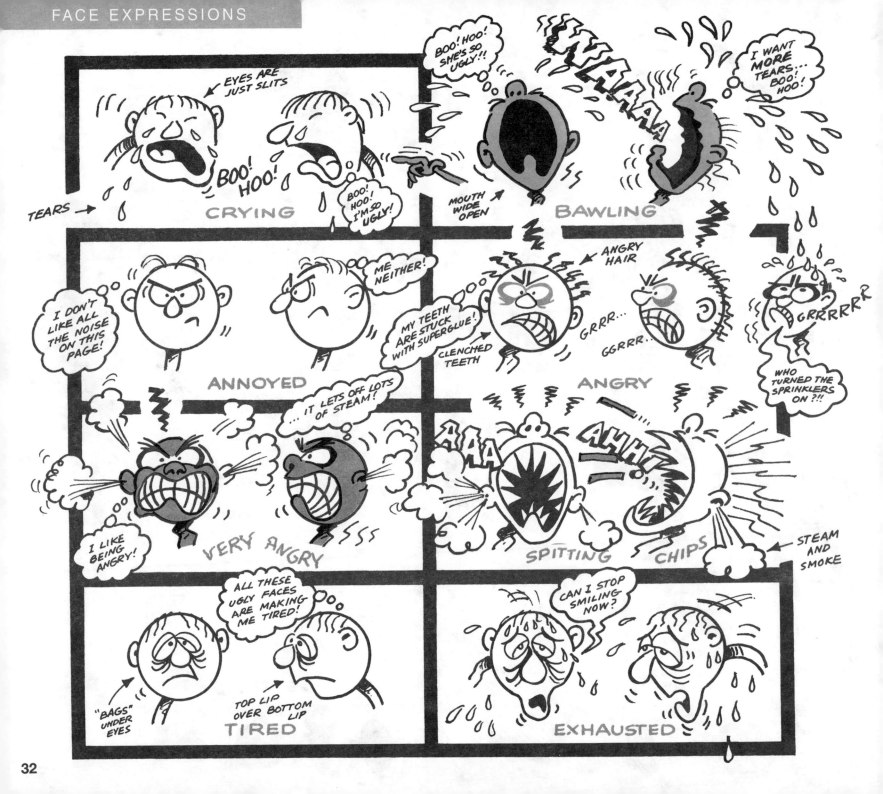

PEOPLE KEEP TURNING OVER THIS PAGE — I NEVER KNOW IF I'M HERE OR THERE!
EYES OVERLAPPING
DIZZY MARKS
DIZZY
SEEING "STARS"
G'DAY!
GIDDY!
WIGGLY MOUTH
DAZED
TONGUE OUT
KNOCKED OUT
FUMES
RED NOSE AND CHEEKS
SEEING "STARS"
DRUNK
BLUSHED CHEEKS
AW, SHUCKS... I CAN'T EVEN LOOK AT HER!
SHAKING MARKS
SHY
HE'S SO CUTE!
BIG TOP EYELIDS
SHOULDER UP
BASHFUL
I WON'T HURT YOU!
WOBBLY EYES
WHA...
WORRIED
EEK! A MOUSE.
SWEAT DROPS
SHIVER AND SHAKE MARKS
NERVOUS

MONEY...
$100
FOOD...
SLURP
SLURP
NICE BIG TONGUE
...I LIKE 'EM BOTH!
GREEDY
NOW, WHERE DID I LEAVE MY WALLET?
I DON'T KNOW.
CONFUSED
DUMB
WE KNOW WHERE HE LEFT HIS WALLET!
WINKING
MMM... WHERE DID HE LEAVE HIS WALLET?
MM...
SUDDEN IDEA (LIGHT BULB GOES ON!)
THINKING HARD
BED
BIG "BAGS" UNDER EYES
I'M TOO TIRED TO THINK!
SLEEPY
HEY! GIVE THAT WALLET BACK!
B-O-R-I-N-G!!
AHH!
YAWNING
986-987-988-999-
SNORING
ASLEEP
BOO!
WHA...
FALSE TEETH
I DREAMED THAT SOMEONE STOLE MY WALLET!
EAR FLYING OFF
WIDE AWAKE AGAIN

Now we'll look at **Types of People** and their **HATS**

On the next few pages we've drawn more than 120 different fairly traditional stereotypes of people.
You might like to change them from, say, a boy to a girl or a woman to a man if you want to — and you can give them a different hairdo or nose shape, hat, etc.

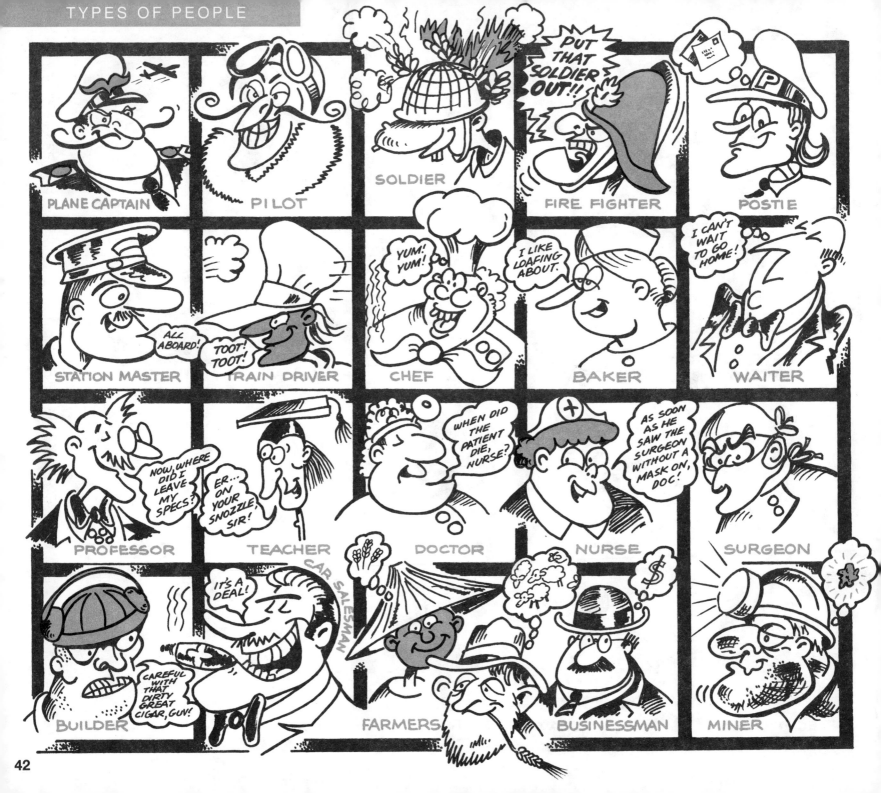

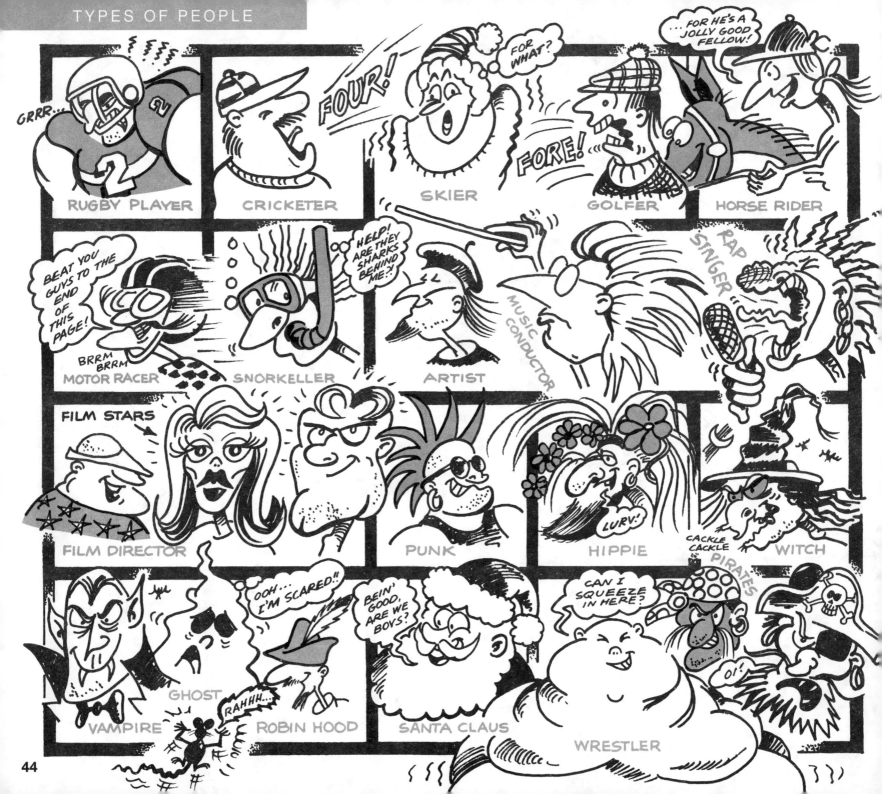

NOW...

I ONLY WANT RESPECTFUL TYPES AT MY SCHOOL!

COMBINE "Types of People" WITH "FACE EXPRESSIONS"

to BRING YOUR CHARACTERS TO LIFE!

FOR EXAMPLE...

A TEACHER **+** A "HAPPY EXPRESSION" **=** A HAPPY TEACHER

OR...

A TEACHER **+** AN "ANGRY EXPRESSION" **=** AN ANGRY TEACHER!

YIKES! I DON'T LIKE THIS TEACHER!

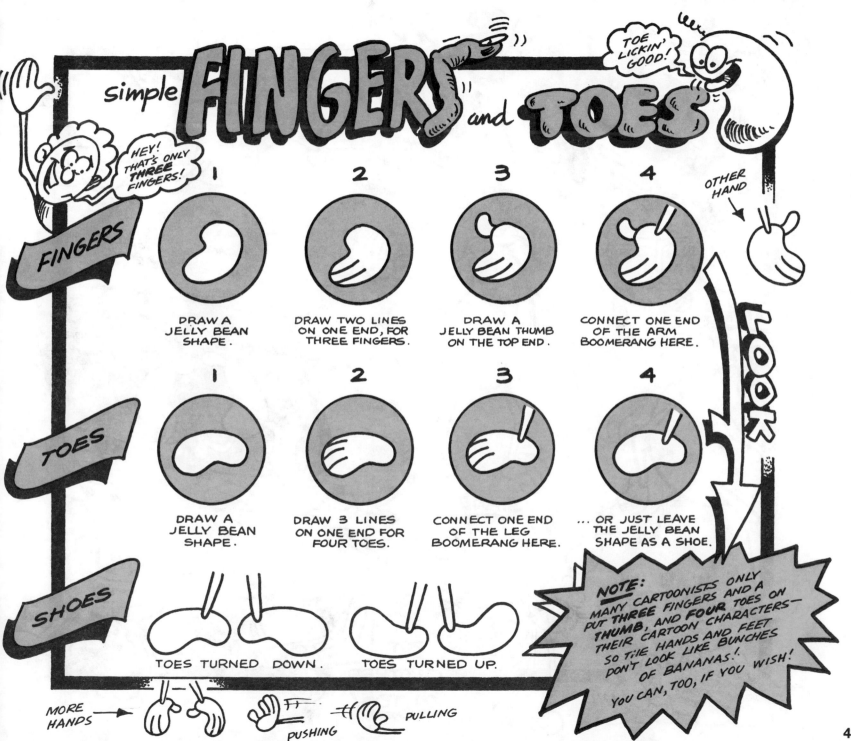

simple **FINGERS** and **TOES**

TOE LICKIN' GOOD!

HEY! THAT'S ONLY **THREE** FINGERS!

FINGERS

OTHER HAND

1 DRAW A JELLY BEAN SHAPE.

2 DRAW TWO LINES ON ONE END, FOR THREE FINGERS.

3 DRAW A JELLY BEAN THUMB ON THE TOP END.

4 CONNECT ONE END OF THE ARM BOOMERANG HERE.

TOES

1 DRAW A JELLY BEAN SHAPE.

2 DRAW 3 LINES ON ONE END FOR FOUR TOES.

3 CONNECT ONE END OF THE LEG BOOMERANG HERE.

4 ... OR JUST LEAVE THE JELLY BEAN SHAPE AS A SHOE.

LOOK

SHOES

TOES TURNED DOWN.

TOES TURNED UP.

NOTE: MANY CARTOONISTS ONLY PUT THREE FINGERS AND A THUMB, AND **FOUR** TOES ON THEIR CARTOON CHARACTERS— SO THE HANDS AND FEET DON'T LOOK LIKE BUNCHES OF BANANAS! YOU CAN, TOO, IF YOU WISH!

MORE HANDS →

PUSHING

PULLING

49

HOW TO DRAW SILLY FACES

DUH...

DON'T WORRY TOO MUCH ABOUT GETTING IT JUST RIGHT— **ANY OLD THING** WILL DO— WE DON'T MIND, DO WE?!

WOBBLY HEAD

WOBBLY NOSE

WIBBLY WOBBLY EYES

CRAZY MOUTH AND TEETH

MAD HAIR

STUPID NECK

IDIOTIC EARS

STICKY OUTY TONGUE

JUST HAVE FUN WITH THESE FACES — THERE ARE **NO RULES**— JUST **DO** IT!"

IF YOU WANT A LONG NOSE... ...**DRAW** A LONG NOSE!

OOH... WHEN WILL IT END?

TEACHER'S BEIN' NOSEY, AGAIN!

51

Caricature...

WHY NOT MAKE ENEMIES OF ALL YOUR FRIENDS — DO A CARICATURE OF THEM ALL!

Caricature is when you look at the main features of a person — and then exaggerate them!

NORMAL	CARTOONISH	NORMAL	CARTOONISH
SAM		MARCI	
LEO		DIANE	
RENÉ		LENA	

BOO, HOO! I'VE BEEN CARICATURED!! WAAAHH...

More **CARICATURE...**

This time, try EXAGGERATING a bit more

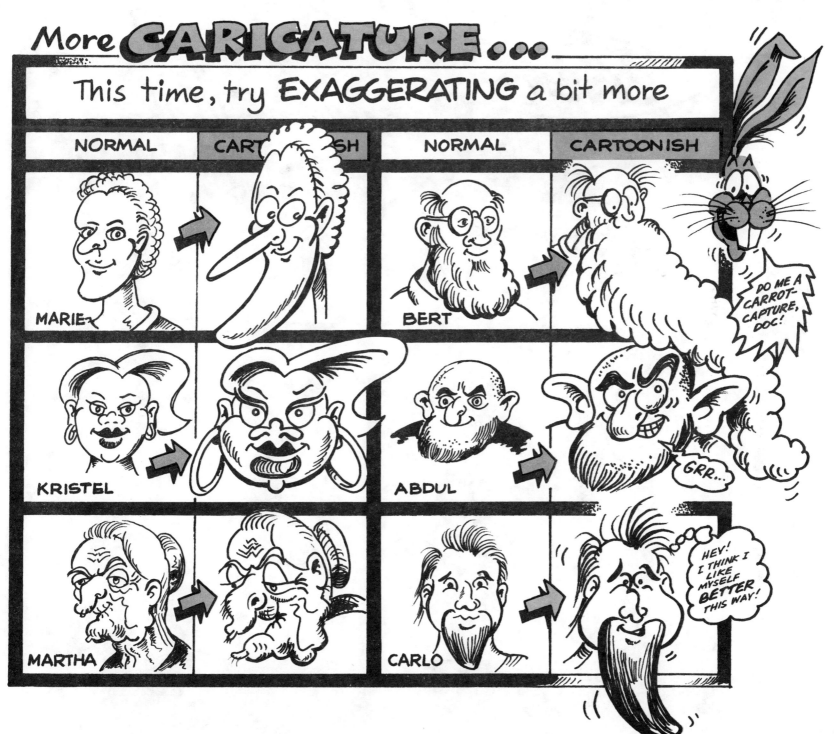

NOTE: IF SOMEONE IS YELLING "HEY!" YOU LOOK UP THE LETTER OF THE ALPHABET THAT RHYMES WITH "HEY" ("A" RHYMES WITH IT) — AND DRAW THAT "FROZEN" MOUTH SHAPE. ANOTHER EXAMPLE: IF A PERSON IS SAYING "NO!" YOU SIMPLY DRAW THE MOUTH AS IF IT'S SAYING THE LETTER "O". GET IT?

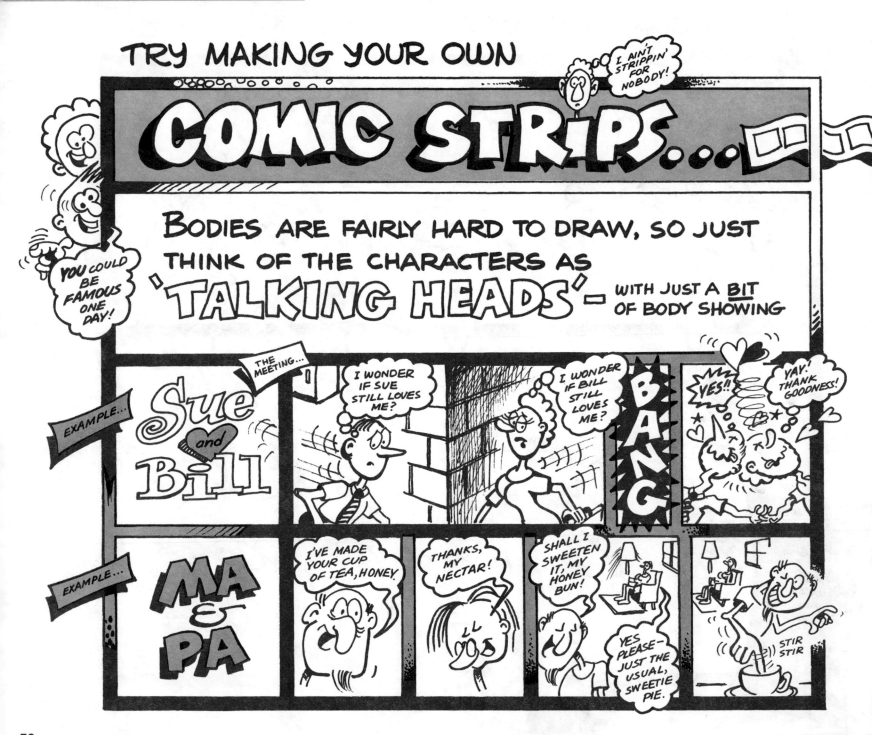

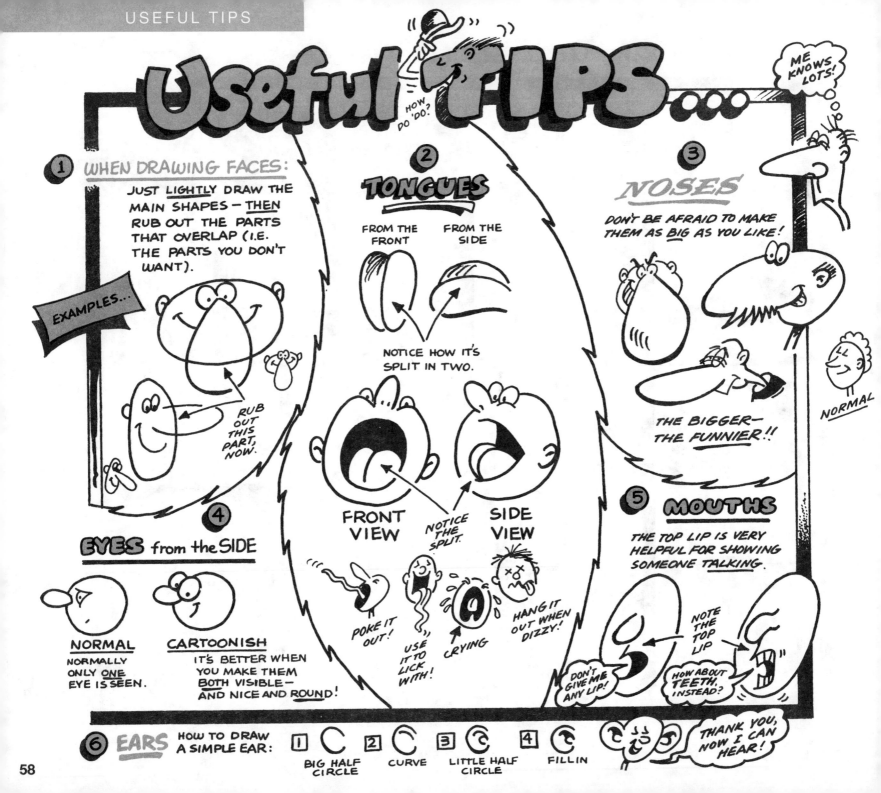

More useful TIPS

THANK YOU!

⑦ **CHEEK LINES**

CHEEK LINES CAN HELP ADD EXPRESSION TO FACES.

EXAMPLES...

CHEEK LINES

⑧ **SHOES**

SIMPLE SHOES

⑨ **PENCILS**

USE REFILLABLE LEAD PENCILS – THEY NEVER GO BLUNT!

WHAT ABOUT ME?

⑩ **ERASERS**

BUY REFILLABLE "PENCIL-ERASERS" – THEY GET INTO HARD-TO-GET-AT PLACES.

COMING TO THE BOIL!!

AIN'T HE UGLY!?

⑪ **USING A MIRROR**

KEEP A SMALL MIRROR BY YOUR DESK. I DID THESE DRAWINGS OF MYSELF BY SIMPLY LOOKING IN THE MIRROR!

FRONT VIEW !!!

SIDE VIEW

CALM   ANNOYED   ANGRY   FUMING   SHOUTING!

NOW...

YOU DO THE SAME, BY LOOKING INTO A MIRROR AT YOURSELF: FROM "CALM TO LAUGHING", FROM "CALM TO CRYING", ETC.

⑫ LAST BUT NOT LEAST: DON'T BE AFRAID TO USE YOUR ERASER! YOU IMPROVE BY SEEING WHAT DOESN'T LOOK RIGHT – AND THEN FIXING IT UP!

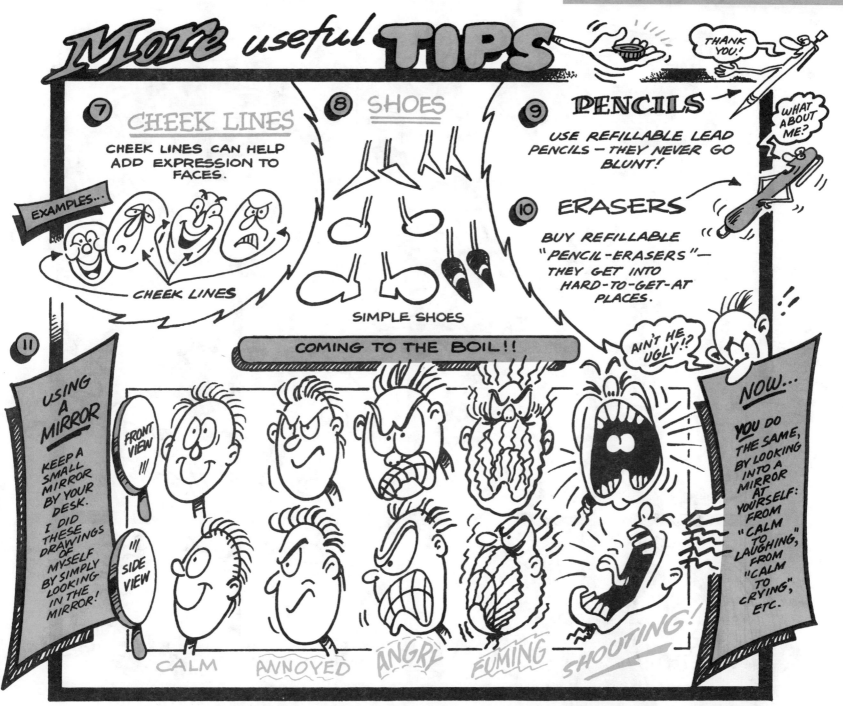

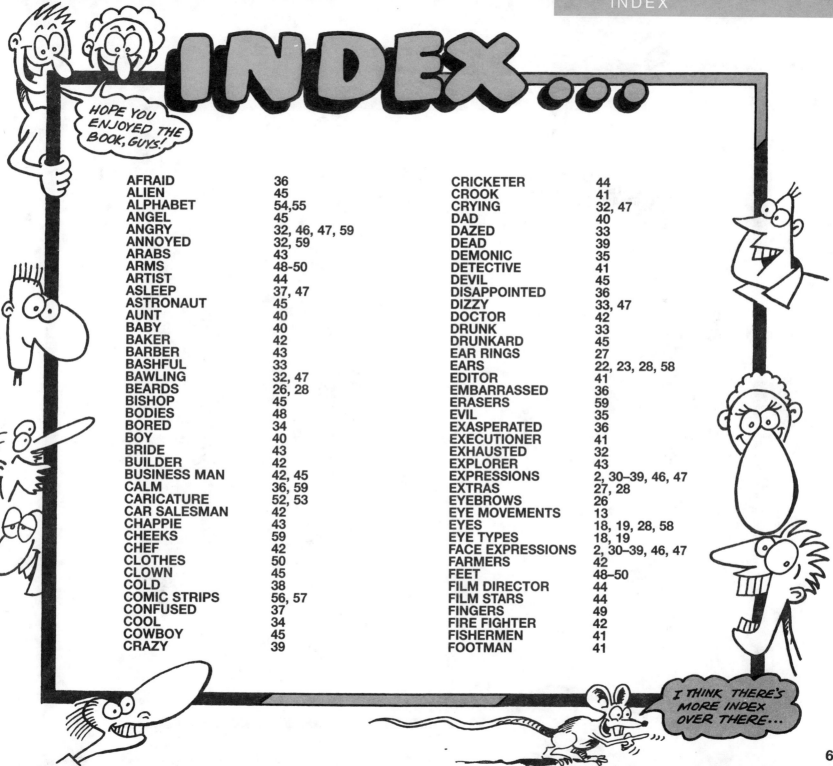

INDEX...

HOPE YOU ENJOYED THE BOOK, GUYS!

I THINK THERE'S MORE INDEX OVER THERE...

HEY, GUYS...
THE INDEX **BEGINS** ON THE PREVIOUS PAGE!

DUH!

GOOD LUCK!

SEE YA!

NICE KNOWING YOU....!